SICK AS A PARROT

SICK AS A PARROT

The World's Worst Jokes

collected by
Nigel Blundell

pictures by
Hilary Hayton

A Piccolo Original
Piccolo Books

First published 1982 by Pan Books Ltd,
Cavaye Place, London SW10 9PG

ISBN 0 330 26588 1
Photoset by Parker Typesetting Service, Leicester
Printed and bound in Great Britain by
Cox & Wyman Ltd, Reading

Contents

Simply Beastly

Son: 'Mum, I've got a new pet goat.'
Mum: 'You can't keep him here, what about the smell?'
Son: 'Oh, the goat won't mind.'

•

After the motorist ran over a small dog, he rushed over to speak to the distinguished-looking woman whose dog it was.

'Ma'am, I will replace your animal.'

'Sir, you flatter yourself,' she replied coldly.

•

A bear went to a building site looking for work. He was given a pick by the foreman and told to start digging. When he went back to work after the tea break, his pick was missing. He went to tell the foreman, and was told: 'Didn't you know, today's the day that teddy bears have their picks nicked!'

•

Two little ants were racing as fast as they could across the top of a cereal box. 'Hey!' puffed one ant. 'What are we running so fast for?' 'Can't you read?' said the other. 'It says right here, tear across the dotted line.'

•

Three budgerigars were in a cage. One was in the top part of the cage, one was in the middle of the cage, and the other one was at the bottom of the cage. Which of the budgies owned the cage?

The one at the bottom. The others were on higher perches.

•

What happened to the cat which ate a ball of wool?

It had mittens.

•

Why did the cat want to join the Red Cross?

It wanted to be a first aid kit.

•

Who wrote the *Thoughts of a China Cat*?

Chairman Miaow.

•

FIRST-AID KIT

SLOW SLOW
QUACK QUACK
SLOW

When is it bad luck to have a black cat follow you?

When you are a mouse.

•

What animal goes hunting mice in the sea?

A catfish.

•

How did a cat win the milk-drinking contest?

It lapped the field.

•

How do ducks dance?

Slow, slow, quack, quack, slow.

•

What is meant by 'illegal'?

A sick bird.

•

What do you call an angry, giant bald eagle?

'Sir'.

•

What are the best steps to take when you meet an escaped lion?

Very long ones.

•

How do you catch a squirrel?

Act like a nut.

•

Why was the sheep arrested by the traffic cop?

For making a ewe-turn.

•

A dog walked into a Wild West saloon with one of its feet bandaged, and six-guns strapped to each back leg. 'What do you want?' asked a cowboy. The dog replied: 'I'm looking for the man who shot m'paw.'

•

What has twelve legs, six ears and one eye?

Three blind mice and half a kipper.

•

What's brown and turns cartwheels?

A brown horse pulling a cart.

•

What sits on a lily pad and says 'cloak, cloak'?

A Chinese flog.

•

How do frogs make beer?

With hops.

•

How do you catch a monkey?

Hang upside down in a tree and make a noise like a banana.

•

What swishes along, making hardly a sound, but leaving holes in your lawn?

A Moles Royce.

•

Why did the chicken stand in the middle of the road?

Because she was a Rhode Island.

•

What is worse than raining cats and dogs?

Hailing taxis.

•

What do you call a parrot with a machine-gun?

A parrot-trooper.

•

Where do you find dinosaurs?

Depends where you leave them.

•

Why did the bald man draw rabbits on his head?

Because, from a distance, they looked like hares.

•

Which key will open no door?

A donkey.

•

What is black and white and red all over?

A sunburned zebra.

•

Where do frogs leave their hats?

In a croakroom.

•

What does a bat sing in the rain?

'Raindrops Keep Falling On My Feet'.

•

What wears a hat and pants?

A well-dressed dog.

•

What do you do with a wombat?

Play wom, of course.

•

What would you call a bald koala?

Fred Bear.

•

Successful bidder (paying auctioneer): 'This is a very expensive parrot. I hope he does talk.'
Parrot (from cage): 'Do I talk? Who do you think was bidding against you?'

•

A man was in his local on Saturday with his dog. When his pal came in with the football results in the evening paper, the dog saw the paper and said: 'Oh no, Barnsley lost again.'

The following Saturday they were in the local again and sure enough the same thing happened. 'Oh no,' said the dog, 'Barnsley lost again.'

'Excuse me,' said another chap who had overheard the dog. 'What does the dog say when Barnsley wins a match?'

'I don't know,' said the owner. 'I've only had him for eight months.'

•

A lady in a shoe department said to the assistant: 'Can I have a pair of crocodile shoes?'

The assistant replied: 'Certainly madam. What size does your crocodile take?'

•

Two caterpillars were sitting on a cabbage leaf when a butterfly flew by. One caterpillar said to the other caterpillar:

'They'll never get me up in one of those things!'

•

The other day I went to the stables to buy a racehorse. The man said: 'I've got just the horse you're looking for.' So I went inside, and there was the horse lying on the floor. When I got the horse outside, it fell down. I said to the man: 'This horse is no good to me. You've got a nice string of horses there. I'll have the one in the middle.' The man said: 'Don't take the one in the middle. He's propping the other ones up.'

•

First man: 'My dog and I go for a tramp in the park every morning.'
Second man: 'I'll bet the dog enjoys it.'
First man: 'Sure does . . . but the tramp's getting a bit fed up.'

•

How do porcupines cuddle each other?

With great care.

•

TICK TOCK
TICK TOCK
WOOF

What goes 'tick-tock, tick-tock, woof'?

A watch dog.

•

A boy walked into a pet shop and said: 'I want a budgie in a hurry, and I'll pay the same price for it that my Mum paid for the Christmas turkey.'

The shopkeeper hurriedly produced a budgie and handed it to the boy.

'Now,' said the man, 'how much did your Mum pay for her turkey?'

'Sixty pence a pound,' said the boy.

•

A man was standing at a bus stop eating fish and chips when a lady with a little dog joined the queue. The dog began to annoy the man by jumping up and trying to beg a chip. Eventually the man said, 'Excuse me, madam, do you mind if I throw your dog a bit?' 'Not at all,' the lady replied. So he threw her dog over the wall.

•

Trainer: 'Did you find your horse well behaved?' Jockey: 'Yes, beautifully mannered. Every time we came to a fence he let me go first.'

•

Why do white sheep eat more than black sheep?

Because there are more white sheep than black sheep.

•

What is a prickly pear?

Two hedgehogs.

•

Why are goats easy to fool?

Because they swallow anything.

•

How do you stop moles digging in the garden?

Hide the spade.

•

Cross Purposes

What do you get if you cross an elephant with a mouse?

Extra-large holes in the skirting board.

•

What do you get when you cross a snake with a Lego set?

A boa constructor.

•

What do you get when you cross a dog with a four-wheeled vehicle?

A Land Rover.

•

What do you get if you cross a hen with a poodle?

Pooched eggs.

•

What do you get if you cross a penguin with a sheep?

A sheepskin dinner jacket.

•

What do you get if you cross a hen with an electric organ?

Hammond eggs.

•

What do you get when you cross a hen with a waiter?

Neatly laid tables.

•

What do you get if you cross an elephant with an abominable snowman?

A jumbo yeti.

•

What do you get if you cross a zebra with a pig?

Striped sausages.

•

What do you get if you cross a bear with a kangaroo?

A fur coat with large pockets.

•

What do you get if you cross William the Conqueror with a power station?

An electricity Bill.

•

What do you get if you cross a tomato with a banana skin?

A pair of red slippers.

•

What do you get if you cross a flea with a rabbit.

Bugs bunny.

•

Irish Antics

Two Irishmen were building a 300-foot chimney. Mick shouted to his mate: 'Bring up the flag, I'm going to put the last coping stone in place.'

His mate shouted back: 'Don't bother, come down here.'

Mick came down and asked: 'What's wrong this time?'

'Well,' came the reply, 'it seems we've got the plans upside-down, it should have been a well!'

•

Have you ever seen an Irish bionic man?

Well, he runs backwards in slow motion.

•

The manager of a cinema said to Paddy: 'That's the fourth ticket you've bought in three minutes.'

'Well,' replied Paddy. 'Inside your cinema there is a stupid girl who's tearing 'em in half!'

•

How do you make an Irishman burn his ear?

Ring him up when he's ironing.

•

How can you spot an Irish executive?

He'll be the one wearing pin-striped wellies!

•

Heard the joke about the Irishman who won the Tour de France? He did a lap of honour!

•

Murphy was engrossed in the crossword. Sucking his pencil, he puzzled over a clue: 'Old Macdonald had one.'

'That's easy,' said Mick. 'It's farm to be sure.'

'How do you spell it?'

'Um . . . E-I-E-I-O . . .' said Mick.

•

An Irishman went to the bar and said: 'Could I have a vodka without orange, please.'

'The barman said: 'We have no orange, only lime.'

'All right,' said the Irishman, 'I'll have it without lime.'

•

HELLO

TREE FELLERS
WANTED

Three Irish labourers were on a building site. One was down a trench digging like mad while the other two stood on the side with their shovels held above their heads.

The foreman stalked up and asked them what they were playing at.

'We are lamposts,' they told him. And he promptly sacked them.

At this, the third labourer jumped out of the trench.

'I didn't mean you,' said the foreman. 'You're all right.'

'You must think I'm daft,' the man replied. 'I'm not working in the dark.'

•

Hear about the Irish goalkeeper who saved a penalty but let it in on the action replay . . .?

•

An Irishman crashed a helicopter. When asked what had gone wrong, he replied: 'I don't know, I'm sure. That blasted fan got on my nerves, so I switched it off.'

•

Mick and Murphy were passing the employment exchange when they saw a sign outside saying: TREE FELLERS WANTED.

'What a shame,' said Mick to Murphy. 'There are only two of us.'

•

Why did the Irish water polo team lose the match?

Their horses drowned.

•

What is written on the top of an Irishman's ladder?

Stop.

•

How do you keep an Irishman busy for hours?

Give him a piece of paper with 'PTO' written on both sides.

•

Why did the Irishman give up his attempt to cross the Atlantic on a plank?

Because he couldn't find a plank long enough.

•

How do you sink an Irish submarine?

Knock on the door.

•

How do Irish dogs get bumps on their heads?

From chasing parked cars.

•

Jumbo Jests

What is the best thing to do if you are chased by an elephant?

Make a trunk call and reverse the charges.

•

What do you call an elephant without ears?

Anything you like – it won't hear you.

•

How do you shoot a pink elephant?

With a pink elephant gun.

•

What is yellow outside, grey inside, and has a great memory?

An elephant omelette.

•

What is white on the outside, grey on the inside, and a meal in itself?

An elephant sandwich.

•

How do you get down from an elephant?

You don't . . . you get down from a duck.

•

Why did the elephant walk on two legs?

To give the ants a better chance.

•

What is the difference between an elephant and a biscuit?

You can't dip an elephant in your coffee.

•

Why is an elephant large, grey and wrinkled?

Because if he was small, round and white, he would be an aspirin.

•

No, seriously, why are elephants grey and wrinkled?

Because they are difficult to iron.

•

JUMBO SNAX

But why are elephants grey?

So as not to confuse them with strawberries.

•

What is big, grey and mutters?

A mumbo jumbo.

•

What did the grape say when the elephant stepped on it?

Nothing. It just let out a little whine.

•

What's the easiest way to catch an elephant?

Chase him up a tree and wait for the fall.

•

How do you tell when you're in bed with an elephant?

By the big 'E' on his pyjama jacket.

•

Food Farces

What's green, hairy and goes up and down all day?

A gooseberry in an elevator.

•

What fruit can be found on a coin?

A date.

•

Why did the orange stop rolling down the hill?

Because it ran out of juice.

•

What sits in a fruit bowl and shouts for help?

A damson in distress.

•

What is rhubarb?

Bloodshot celery.

•

What can you make with two banana skins?

A pair of slippers.

•

What would you do if you found a blue banana?

Try to cheer it up.

•

What is green and white and bounces?

A spring onion.

•

Why is bread like Champagne?

It is good for toasting.

•

Why did the man eat little bits of metal all day?

Because he was on a staple diet.

•

Why did the biscuit box?

Because it saw the rum punch.

•

What do you feed to undernourished dwarfs?

Elf-raising flour.

•

Is sherry the best drink for seasickness?

No, port is better.

•

What is brown, sticky and shocking?

Electric treacle.

•

What is yellow and flat and goes round at 33⅓ revolutions per minute?

A long-playing omelette.

•

What book is full of stirring chapters?

A cookery book.

•

What is yellow and white and travels at 100 miles an hour?

A train driver's egg sandwich.

•

What is white and fluffy and swings through the jungle?

A meringue-outang.

•

What is yellow and explodes over your pudding?

Kamikaze custard.

•

What has knobs on and wobbles?

Jellyvision.

•

When is soup musical?

When it is piping hot.

•

What is a lawyer's favourite pudding?

Sue-it.

•

What is thin, cowardly and full of noodles?

Chicken soup.

•

What stays hot in a refrigerator?

Mustard.

•

A traveller arrived at a cafe and asked if he could have his thermos flask filled with three cups of tea.

As an afterthought he added: 'Make that two with sugar and one without.'

•

Into the bar walked a man with jelly and cream in one ear. The barman said to him, 'Excuse me, sir, do you know you've got jelly and cream in one ear?'

The man replied, 'You'll have to speak up, I'm a trifle deaf.'

•

'Waiter, waiter, there's a button in my lunch.'
'That's the chef's fault, he cooked the potatoes with their jackets on.'

•

'Waiter, waiter, do you have frogs' legs?'
'No, sir, I always walk like this.'

•

'Waiter, waiter, is the soup thick?'
'It looks really stupid to me, sir.'

•

'Waiter, waiter, what's this twig doing on my plate?'
'I'll ask the branch manager, sir.'

•

'Waiter, waiter, this coffee tastes like mud.'
'I'm not surprised, sir, it was only ground this morning.'

•

'Waiter, waiter, I can't see any chicken in my chicken and ham pie.'
'Well, sir, you wouldn't expect to find a dog in a dog biscuit, would you?'

•

'Waiter, waiter, this stew isn't fit for a pig to eat.'
'I'll take it back, sir, and bring you one that is.'

•

'Waiter, waiter, there's a fly in my soup.'
'No, sir, that's the cook. The last customer was a witch-doctor.'

•

'Waiter, waiter, there are *two* flies in my soup.'
'It's a special offer, sir.'

•

Waiter: 'How did you find the steak, sir?'
Diner: 'I lifted up a mushroom, and there it was!'

•

Alf: 'Have you see today's newspaper?'
Bert: 'No, what was in it?'
Alf: 'My lunch.'

•

PORKERS

MACAW

Scatty Scots

Notice in Scottish golf club: 'Members are requested not to pick up lost balls until they have stopped moving.'

•

Ma: 'What are we getting wee Donald for Christmas?'
Pa: 'You remember that balloon we got him last Christmas?'
Ma: 'Yes.'
Pa: 'We'll blow it up for him this Christmas.'

•

What is a macaw?

A Scottish parrot.

•

Which Scottish regiment goes 'tick-tock' in the dark?

The Black Watch.

•

What do you call Scottish shellfish?

The Clam McCrab.

•

Why wouldn't the Scotsman allow his daughter to get married?

Because he'd have to give her away.

•

What do Scotsmen have after the main course?

Tart-an custard.

•

Really Silly Stuff

Why was Goldilocks from such a small family?

Because she had three bears but everyone else has forebears.

•

Who invented the first fireplace?

Alfred the Grate.

•

Why does Father Christmas go down the chimney?

Because it soots him.

•

Who is Wyatt Burp?

The sheriff with a repeater.

•

Why did Simple Simon put corn in his shoes?

Because of his pigeon toes.

•

What did Dick Turpin say at the end of his famous ride to York?

'Whoa.'

•

How did Little Bo Peep lose her sheep?

She had a crook with her.

•

Who was the most popular actor in the Bible?

Samson – he brought the house down.

•

What is round, has teeth and bites?

A vicious circle.

•

Why is draughts a dangerous game?

Because you could catch a chill.

•

Why are footballers happy people?

Because they get a kick out of their jobs.

•

What is round, red and rude?

Tomato sauce.

•

What is smelly and comes out shooting?

A septic tank.

•

What is white and gives milk but has only one horn?

A milk truck.

•

What do you call an Arab milkman?

A milk Sheik.

•

If you have a referee in football and boxing, what do you have in bowls?

Soup.

•

Why are sports grounds always windy?

Because there are so many fans.

•

What do you call a heavyweight Egyptian motor mechanic?

Two-ton-car-man.

•

MILK SHEIK

What sits on the lawn going 'tick-tock-tick-tock'?

A metrognome.

•

Why do traffic wardens have yellow lines on their hats?

To stop people from parking on their heads.

•

Where do astronauts leave their spaceships?

At parking meteors.

•

What was awarded to the inventor of door knockers?

The No-Bell Prize.

•

How do you make a bandstand?

Take all the chairs away.

•

Pure Corn

An out-of-work man went into a railway booking office and asked for a single ticket to Jeopardy.

The clerk looked through his books, and said: 'Are you sure that's the right name?'

The man took the clerk on to the platform, and pointed to a newspaper poster. It read: *10,000 car jobs in jeopardy*.

•

Boating lake attendant: 'Come in boat No. 99.'
Boating lake manager: 'We haven't got a boat No. 99.'
Attendant: 'Boat No. 66 – are you in trouble?'

•

A car with three convicts collided with a cement mixer. Now police are hunting three hardened criminals.

•

An old Knight returning from the wars, came to grief in the snow. His horse ran off, leaving him exhausted in the mountains. A St Bernard dog rescued him. The Knight climbed on his back and away they went down the mountain.

A storm blew up when at last they came to a farmhouse. Still astride the dog, the Knight knocked on the door and the farmer opened the door and said: 'Cor, I can't turn a Knight away on a dog like this.'

•

Sir Galahad and Sir Lancelot were riding along a dusty road when they spotted an ice cream seller. Sir Galahad bought a large cone and walked away licking it appreciatively. Sir Lancelot dismounted and also asked for an ice cream. But the ice cream salesman said: 'Sorry, I can't serve you. This is only a one Knight stand.'

•

Why did the golfer carry a spare pair of trousers?

In case he got a hole in one.

•

What is yellow, has twenty-two legs and goes 'clunch, clunch, clunch'?

A Chinese football team eating crisps.

•

What do you find on Peking Golf Course?

China tees.

•

Who was the fastest runner on Earth?

Adam – he was first in the human race.

•

What game do horses play?

Stable tennis.

•

What car starts with T?

None, they all need petrol.

•

What's black and white and goes at sixty miles per hour.

A vicar on a motorbike.

•

What plays snuffly rock music?

Electric catarrh.

•

What is the best hat for musicians?

Any hat with a band on it.

•

What did the drill say to the hammer?

'I've got such a boring job.'

•

What did the fuse say to the electrician?

'Send me a wire.'

•

More corn. . .

Door numbers have been stolen from 6 Acton Lane, 66 London Road and 666 Brighton Avenue. Police believe this to be the work of a six maniac.

•

Did you hear about the cargo ship that sank nineteen times? It was carrying yo-yos.

•

What did Big Chief Running Water call his two sons?

Hot and Cold.
And what did he call his third son?
Little Drip.

•

An American who didn't understand English money arrived at Heathrow Airport. A young lad said to him: 'Can I carry your bags for 50p, sir?'

'What's 50p?' asked the Yank.

'I agree,' said the lad. 'Make it £2.'

•

A stranger in a small village asked one of the locals: 'Excuse me, sir, do you happen to know a man with one leg called Thomson?'

'I'm not sure,' replied the local. 'What's the name of his other leg?'

•

Have you heard the one about the three boiled eggs?

Two bad.

•

Have you heard about the tycoon who ordered his chauffeur: 'Drive over the cliff – I'm committing suicide'?

•

Have you heard the one about the big wall?

Sorry, can't tell you – you'll never get over it.

•

Have you heard about the racing driver who ran out of fuel?

He refused to pull into the pits because no one was offering Trading Stamps.

•

What did the two cloud convenors say to one another?

'Let's have a lightning strike.'

•

What did one lion say to the other lion as two hunters drove up in a Jeep?

'Here come Meals on Wheels.'

•

Where do you get trees from?

The tree shop, they have branches everywhere.

•

What's purple and round, and floats up in the sky?

The Planet of the Grapes.

•

How do you avoid that run-down feeling?

Look both ways before crossing the road.

•

Which insect eats the least?

The moth, it just eats holes.

•

What's good for flat feet?

A foot pump.

•

Did you hear the one about the blunt pencil?

There's no point to it.

•

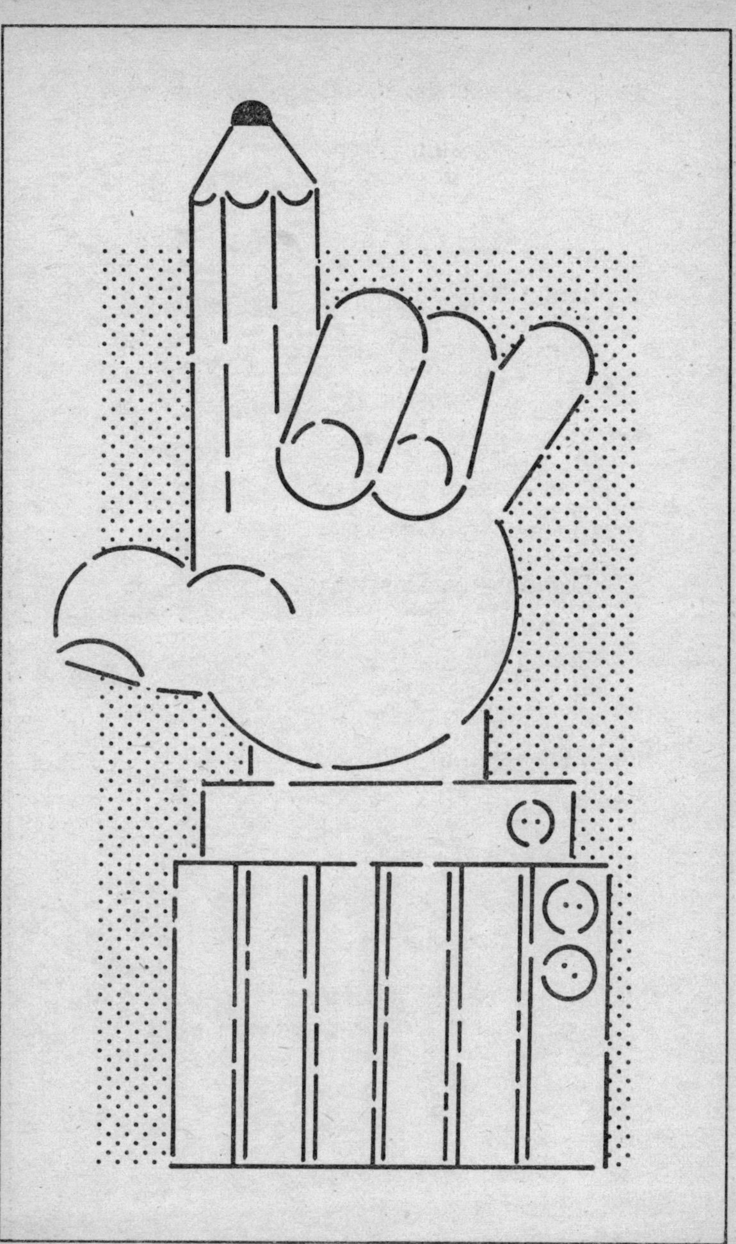

Why is it hard to try and keep a secret in winter?

Because your teeth chatter.

•

Why wouldn't the steam train engine sit down?

Because it had a tender behind.

•

What do you call a big game hunter?

Someone who lost his way to the match.

•

What swings through the trees carrying a briefcase?

A branch manager.

•

What goes 'peck-peck-peck-bang'?

A chicken in a mine-field.

•

Who tells chicken jokes?

Comedihens.

•

What is black, out of its mind and sits in trees?

A raven lunatic.

•

Do you need training to be a litter collector?

No, you just pick it up as you go along.

•

What has two legs, one wheel and flies?

A wheelbarrow full of manure.

•

How do you avoid falling hair?

Get out of the way.

•

What's white and goes up?

A stupid snowflake.

•

What goes 'ha-ha-ha-bonk'?

A man laughing his head off.

•

Why can't your nose be twelve inches long?

Because it would be a foot.

•

What are hippies for?

To hang your leggies on.

•

What is black and rushes out of the ground shouting 'Knickers!'?

Crude oil.

•

What is black and rushes out of the ground shouting 'Underwear'?

Refined oil.

•

What happened to the man who stole a calendar?

He got twelve months.

•

What do you call a clock on the Moon?

A luna-tic.

•

What is a horse's best friend?

His neigh-bour.

•

What did the policeman say to his chest?

'You are under a vest.'

•

Why is 'smiles' the world's longest word?

Because there is a mile between the first and last letters.

•

What is the best way to light a fire with two sticks?

Make sure one of them is a match.

•

Something Completely Different

What is the difference between a camera and the measles?

One makes facsimilies and the other makes sick families.

•

What is the difference between a candle in a cave and a dance in an inn?

One is a taper in a cavern and the other a caper in a tavern.

•

What is the difference between an angry circus owner and a Roman barber?

One is a raving showman and the other is a shaving Roman.

•

What is the difference between Mount Everest and cod liver oil?

One is hard to get up, the other is hard to get down.

•

What is the difference between a weasel and a stoat?

One is weasily distinguished, and the other is stoatally different.

•

What is the difference between a sick elephant and a dead bee?

One is a seedy beast, and the other is a bee deceased.

•

What is the difference between a leopard and a comma?

One has claws at the end of its paws, and the other is a pause at the end of a clause.

•

What is the difference between a hairdresser and a sculptor?

A hairdresser curls up and dyes while a sculptor makes faces and busts.

•

What is the difference between a flying saucer and a school sausage?

One is an Unidentified Flying Object and the other is an Unidentifiable Frying Object.

•

What is the difference between a wet day and a lion with toothache?

One is pouring with rain, the other is roaring with pain.

•

Why was the lone yachtsman disqualified from the single-handed ocean race?

Because he used both hands.

•

What was the crooked orchestra leader charged with?

Robbery with violins.

•

What goes 'moooz'?

A plane flying upside down.

•

What makes a man mean?

The letter E.

•

Why are feet like ancient tales?

They are both leg-ends.

•

Why is a rock braver than a mountain?

Because it is a little boulder.

•

What fruit grows on telegraph poles?

Electric currants.

•

Fishy Tales

What dashes round the sea bed chasing crooks?

A squid car.

•

Who was the world's first underwater spy?

James Pond.

•

Which American President lived beside the sea and ate people?

Jaws Washington.

•

What stops off at the bottom of the ocean with sixty people on board?

An octobus.

•

What is twenty-five feet long, ugly and sings 'Scotland the Brave'?

The Loch Ness Songster.

•

What has eight guns and terrorizes the ocean deep?

Billy the Squid.

•

What do you call a neurotic octopus?

A crazy mixed-up squid.

•

What has eighty-eight black-and-white teeth and roams the ocean?

A piano tuna.

•

What leaves yellow footprints all over the sea bed?

A lemon sole.

•

What swims through the water at 100 miles an hour?

A motorpike.

•

What lives under the water and goes 'Dit-dit-da-da-dit'?

A Morse cod.

•

What would Neptune say if the sea dried up?

I haven't a notion.

•

What terrorizes other fish at the bottom of the sea?

Jack the Kipper.

•

What fish wears spurs and a cowboy hat?

Billy the Cod.

•

What lurks at the bottom of the sea and makes you an offer you can't refuse?

The Codfather.

•

Mother: 'Have you given the goldfish fresh water today?'
Billy: 'No. They haven't finished the water I gave them yesterday.'

•

Quirky Quotes

Dad: 'Peter, who gave you that black eye?
Peter: 'Nobody gave it to me, Dad. I had to fight for it.'

•

'Guilty or not guilty?' the judge asked the defendant.
'How would I know that?', came the reply; 'I haven't heard the evidence yet.'

•

Lady to a tramp who has asked for a meal: 'Do you like a cold rice pudding?'
Tramp: 'I love it, lady.'
Lady: 'Well, call back later, because it's very hot right now.'

•

'My mother is really silly. I told her I had grown another foot since I joined the Army and she's sent me another sock!'

•

Actor: 'I hate to criticize, but that baby playing Moses as an infant is terrible.'
Director: 'I know. I can't understand it, he was great in the rushes.'

•

'Have you got any books with a good mystery ending?'
Librarian: 'Yes, here's one with the last chapter torn out.'

•

John: 'Does your watch tell the time?'
Jim: 'No, you have to look at it.'

•

Sergeant to paratrooper who has just jumped from a plane: 'Why haven't you got a parachute?'
Soldier: 'It's OK, sarge, we're only practising.'

•

BILL
Mr. WEBB

There was a man standing at the bus stop with two eyes, no arms and one leg. When the bus came the conductor said: 'Eye, eye, you look 'armless, 'op on.'

•

A notice in the foyer of a cinema said: 'Old Age Pensioners admitted free if accompanied by their Parents.'

•

Pat: 'Who are the crowd booing?'
Mick: 'The man who threw the brick at the ref.'
Pat: 'But it missed.'
Mick: 'That's why they're booing.'

•

Little boy: 'Dad, there's a man at the door with a bill.'
Father: 'It can't be, it must be a duck with a hat on!'

•

Prof. Prune: 'I swallowed some uranium.'
Prof. Plum: 'What happened?'
Prof. Prune: 'I got atomic ache!'

•

Football manager: 'Why do you call our goalkeeper Cinderella?'
Player: 'Because he's always missing the ball.'

•

A raider went into a bank with his hand in his pocket and said to the clerk: 'Put your hands in the air, this is a muck up.'
Clerk: 'Excuse m-me, s-sir, don't you mean a stick-up?'
Raider: 'No. I mean a muck-up. I left my gun at home.'

•

Psychiatrist to patient: 'My dear sir, you are not suffering from an inferiority complex – you are inferior!'

•

Maniac Medicine

A man was lying in hospital after a road accident. A doctor came up to him and said: 'I have some good news and some bad news for you.

'The bad news is that we've cut both your legs off. The good news is that the chap in the next bed wants to buy your slippers.'

•

'Doctor, doctor, I just can't stop my hands shaking.'
Doctor: 'Do you drink much?'
'Not really. I seem to spill most of it.'

•

'Doctor, doctor, I've just swallowed a sheep.'
'How do you feel?'
'Very ba-a-a-ad.'

•

'Doctor, doctor, this cream makes my arm smart.'
Doctor: 'You should rub some on your head then!'

•

'Doctor, doctor, I keep thinking I'm a door.'
'Doctor: 'I think this could be an open and shut case.'

•

'Doctor, doctor, I keep feeling like a parachute.'
Doctor: 'Do drop in any time.'

•

'Doctor, doctor, I think I'm suffering from amnesia.'
'Take these pills, and you'll soon forget all about it.'

•

'Doctor, doctor, your cure didn't work.'
Doctor: 'Did you drink a glass of orange juice after a hot bath?
'No, after drinking the hot bath, I didn't feel like drinking the orange juice!'

•

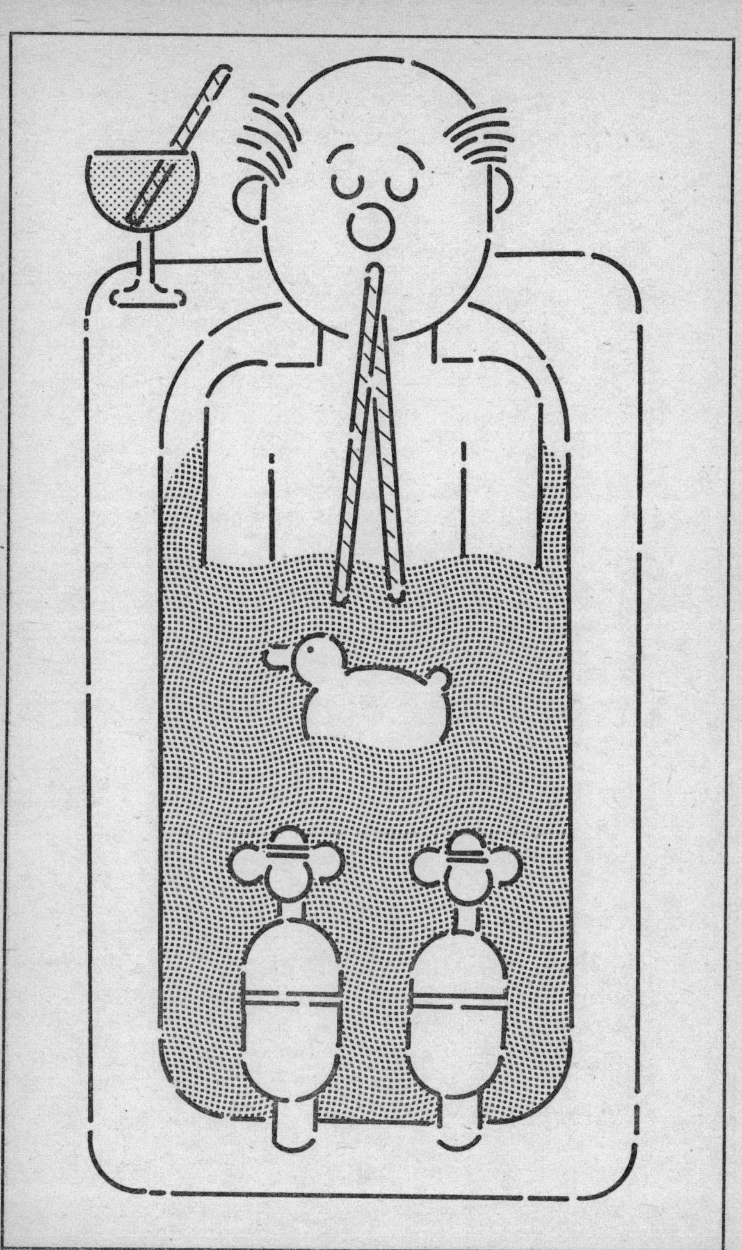

'Doctor, doctor, I feel like custard.'
'Sit down, man, and don't be so thick.'

•

'Doctor, doctor, as soon as I've said something, I forget it.'
Doctor: 'How long has this been going on?'
Patient: 'How long has what been going on?'

•

Doctor: 'I think you have acute appendicitis.'
Patient: 'Thanks, doc, I'm glad you like it.'

•

'Doctor, doctor, I've been stung by a bee.'
'Shall I put some cream on it?'
'Don't be silly, it must be miles away by now.'

•

'Doctor, doctor, I feel like a cup of tea.'
'What's got into you?'
'Milk and two sugars!'

•

'Doctor, doctor, every time I drink a cup of tea, I get a pain in my right eye.'
Doctor: 'Take the spoon out of the cup before you drink next time.'

•

'Doctor, doctor, I've swallowed a spoon!'
'Well, sit down there, and don't stir.'

•

'Doctor, doctor, I keep thinking I'm a bridge.'
'What came over you?'
'Two buses, three cars and a lorry!'

•

'Doctor, doctor, I keep thinking I'm still at school!'
'Sit down and I'll give you an examination.'

•

Doctor: 'You look very flushed, you must have flu.'
Patient: 'No, I walked.'

•

12
1
2
3
4
5
6
7
8
9
10
11
JUST A SECOND

'Doctor, doctor, I can't stop stealing things.'
Doctor: 'Try these pills for a week. And if they don't work, try to get me a colour telly.'

•

'Doctor, doctor, I keep thinking I'm a car.'
Doctor: 'You must be going round the bend by now.'

•

'Doctor, doctor, I'm worried about my fifteen-year-old boy – he weighs twenty stone and is seven feet tall.'
Doctor: 'Don't worry, lady, he'll grow out of it.'

•

'Doctor, doctor, I keep thinking I'm a clock.'
Doctor: 'I expect you're a little wound up.'

•

Vladimir Koziakin
Superworld Mazes 95p

The Cyborg missions have attacked the human colonies – you have 4 minutes 45 seconds to get them out of danger! Which route? Can you do it? Will you be able to save the humans or will they fall into the evil clutches of rogue Cyborgs, or plunge deep into the whirling vortex of space? It's a risk – solve the maze puzzles and you will live to fight again.

Eva Ibbotson
Which Witch? £1.25

Old Mother Bloodwort (all warts and whiskers), Ethel Feedbag (smelly wellington wearer), Mable Wrack (daughter of a mermaid, teller of fishy tales), Nora and Nancy Shouter, Madam Olympia (the blackest witch ever), Belladonna (once white – she has never recovered) – which witch will be eligible to marry Arriman, awful wizard of the North? The competition begins as each witch in turn pulls out of the cauldron her specially evil spell – but some spells go terribly, unspeakably, horribly wrong . . .